NEW MOON OF THE SEASONS

NEW MOON
OF THE SEASONS

Prayers from the Highlands and Islands

Collected and translated by
ALEXANDER CARMICHAEL

Selected by
MICHAEL JONES

LINDISFARNE PRESS

The title is from
'The New Moon' p. 122

These verses are selected from the *Carmina Gadelica* published in six volumes between 1900 and 1961.

This edition published in 1992 by
Lindisfarne Press, RR4, Box 94A-1, Hudson, NY 12534

ISBN 0-940262-51-7

Printed in Great Britain
by Dotesios Ltd, Trowbridge, Wilts.

CONTENTS

Foreword   9

Morning Protection

Prayer   13
Prayer at Rising   14
God's Aid   15
Prayer at Rising   16
Morning Prayer   17

Journeys on Land and Sea

The Pilgrim's Aiding   21
The Prayer   22
The Aiding   23
The Gospel of Christ   24
The Gospel of the God of Life   27
Prayer for Travelling   28

Work

Kindling the Fire   31
Smooring the Fire   32
Milking Song   33
Ho, my Heifer!   34
Herding Blessing   35
Marking the Lambs   36
Blessing   37
The Chant of the Warping   38
The Consecration of the Cloth   40
Consecration of the Cloth   41
Hunting Blessing   42
Consecrating the Chase   44
Choice of Timber   45
Choice   45
Fishing Blessing   46
The Ocean Blessing   48
Ocean Blessing   50

Charms and Banishings

Charm for Fear by Night	53
God of the Moon, God of the Sun	54
Thwarting the Eye	55
Exorcism of the Eye	56
Spell of the Eye	58
Charm against Venom	59
Charm against Women	60
Prayer	61
Good Wish	62
The Yarrow	63
The Yarrow	64
The Aspen	65
Silverweed	66
The Charm of the Figwort	67
St Columba's Plant	68
The Shamrock of Power	69

Encompassing

Encompassing	73
The Three	74
Encompassing	75
Encompassment	76
Grace	77
Prayer of Protection	78
Jesus the Encompasser	79
The Pilgrim's Safeguarding	80
Thou, my Soul's Healer	81

Prayers and Blessings

Holy Father of Glory	85
The Three	86
Prayer	87
A Prayer for Grace	88
Invocation for Justice	89
A Resting Prayer	90
House Protecting	91
The Meal	92

Prayer of Distress 93
Blessings 94

Festivals and Saints

The First Miracle of Christ 101
Christmas Carol 103
The Child of Glory 105
Christmas Chant 106
The Blessing of the New Year 108
God of the Moon 109
Saint Brigit 110
The Beltane Blessing 112
Michael of the Angels 114
To Whom Shall I Offer Oblation? 115
Soul Peace 116
Brian 117

Moon

Moon Worship 121
The New Moon 122
Queen of the Night 123
Beauteous Fair One of Grace 124
New Moon 125
The New Moon 126

Mary

A Prayer 129
Prayer to Mary Mother 130
Praise of Mary 135

Sleep Protection

Prayer 139
Thou Great God 140
Sleep Consecration 141
I Lie down this Night 142
Soul-Shrine 143
Petition 144
I Lie in my Bed 145
Sleep Blessing 146

Night Prayer   147
Rest Benediction   148
Repose of Sleep   149
The Dedication   150

Death Blessing

The Death Dirge   153
The Day of Death   154
Death   155
Death Prayer   156
Joyous Death   157
The Battle to Come   158
Supplication   159

Sources   160

FOREWORD

Alexander Carmichael collected and translated these prayers during the last half of the nineteenth century. He travelled through the Highlands and Islands of Scotland where they were still remembered, winning the trust and respect of the men and women who had them by heart. He was of the opinion that he had not done justice to the original Gaelic but was encouraged, especially by his wife, to continue with this work.

I first met these 'Hymns and Incantations' through the anthology, *The Sun Dances*, made by Adam Bittleston. This drew me to Carmichael's complete *Carmina Gadelica*. Although Bittleston had taken many of the pearls for *The Sun Dances* there was still an incredible wealth of material, easily enough for another collection. I could be bold in my selection as there is now a much greater awareness of the importance of the spirituality expressed in these beautiful Celtic prayers. Many of them have remnants of the ancient tradition of the bards, who knew how to form words into incantations to heal, bless and protect. Although today, perhaps, we do not need protection so much from the powers in fire, wind, rain and rock, the elements within continue to rage ferociously. The recognition of having fallen away from God, from the basis of all harmony, is very strong in many of these prayers. It is out of this pain that some of the most triumphant and intimate invocations of Christ ever made have arisen.

Michael Jones

Morning Protection

PRAYER

Thanks to Thee ever, O gentle Christ,
  That Thou hast raised me freely from the black
And from the darkness of last night
  To the kindly light of this day.

Praise unto Thee, O God of all creatures,
  According to each life Thou hast poured on me,
My desire, my word, my sense, my repute,
  My thought, my deed, my way, my fame.

PRAYER AT RISING

Bless to me, O God,
  Each thing mine eye sees;
Bless to me, O God,
  Each sound mine ear hears;
Bless to me, O God,
  Each odour that goes to my nostrils;
Bless to me, O God,
  Each taste that goes to my lips;
  Each note that goes to my song,
  Each ray that guides my way,
  Each thing that I pursue,
  Each lure that tempts my will,
  The zeal that seeks my living soul,
The Three that seek my heart,
  The zeal that seeks my living soul,
The Three that seek my heart.

GOD'S AID

God to enfold me,
   God to surround me,
God in my speaking,
   God in my thinking.

God in my sleeping,
   God in my waking,
God in my watching,
   God in my hoping.

God in my life,
   God in my lips,
God in my soul,
   God in my heart.

God in my sufficing,
   God in my slumber,
God in mine ever-living soul,
   God in mine eternity.

PRAYER AT RISING

Thou King of moon and sun,
  Thou King of stars,
Thou Thyself knowest our need,
  O Thou merciful God of life.

Each day that we move,
  Each time that we awaken,
Causing vexation and gloom
  To the King of hosts Who loved us.

Be with us through each day,
  Be with us through each night;
Be with us each night and day,
  Be with us each day and night.

MORNING PRAYER

Bless to me, O God,
  My soul and my body;
Bless to me, O God,
  My belief and my condition;

Bless to me, O God,
  My heart and my speech,
And bless to me, O God,
  The handling of my hand;

  Strength and busyness of morning,
  Habit and temper of modesty,
  Force and wisdom of thought,
  And Thine own path, O God of virtues,
    Till I go to sleep this night;

Thine own path, O God of virtues,
  Till I go to sleep this night.

Journeys on Land and Sea

THE PILGRIMS' AIDING

God be with thee in every pass,
Jesus be with thee on every hill,
Spirit be with thee on every stream,
    Headland and ridge and lawn;

Each sea and land, each moor and meadow,
Each lying down, each rising up,
In the trough of the waves, on the crest of the
                                  billows,
    Each step of the journey thou goest.

THE PRAYER

I am praying and appealing to God,
The Son of Mary and the Spirit of truth,
To aid me in distress of sea and of land:
May the Three succour me, may the Three shield
me,
    May the Three watch me by day and by night.

God and Jesus and the Spirit of cleansing
Be shielding me, be possessing me, be aiding me,
Be clearing my path and going before my soul
In hollow, on hill, on plain,
    On sea and land be the Three aiding me.

God and Jesus and the Holy Spirit
Be shielding and saving me,
As Three and as One,
By my knee, by my back, by my side,
    Each step of the stormy world.

THE AIDING

May Brigit shield me,
May Mary shield me,
May Michael shield me,
  On sea and on land:
    To shield me from all anguish
  On sea and on land,
    To shield me from all anguish.

May Father aid me,
May Son aid me,
May Spirit aid me,
  On sea and on land:
    In the shielding of the City everlasting
  On sea and on land,
    In the shielding of the City everlasting.

May the Three succour me,
May the Three follow me,
May the Three guide me,
  On sea and on land,
    To the Vine-garden of the godlike
  On sea and on land,
    To the Vine-garden of the godlike.

THE GOSPEL OF CHRIST

May God bless thy cross
　　Before thou go over the sea;
Any illness that thou mayest have,
　　It shall not take thee hence.

May God bless thy crucifying cross
　　In the house-shelter of Christ,
Against drowning, against peril, against spells,
　　Against sore wounding, against grisly fright.

As the King of kings was stretched up
　　Without pity, without compassion, to the tree,
The leafy, brown, wreathed topmost Bough,
　　As the body of the sinless Christ triumphed,

And as the woman of the seven blessings,
　　Who is going in at their head,
May God bless all that are before thee
　　And thee who art moving anear them.

　　　　Grace of form,
　　　　　Grace of voice be thine;
　　　　Grace of charity,
　　　　　Grace of wisdom be thine;
　　　　Grace of beauty,
　　　　　Grace of health be thine;
　　　　Grace of sea,
　　　　　Grace of land be thine;
　　　　Grace of music,
　　　　　Grace of guidance be thine;

Grace of battle-triumph,
    Grace of victory be thine;
Grace of life,
    Grace of praise be thine;
Grace of love,
    Grace of dancing be thine;
Grace of lyre,
    Grace of harp be thine;
Grace of sense,
    Grace of reason be thine;
Grace of speech,
    Grace of story be thine;
Grace of peace,
    Grace of God be thine.

A voice soft and musical I pray for thee,
    And a tongue loving and mild:
Two things good for daughter and for son,
    For husband and for wife.

The joy of God be in thy face,
    Joy to all who see thee;
The circling of God be keeping thee,
    Angels of God shielding thee.

        Nor sword shall wound thee,
        Nor brand shall burn thee,
        Nor arrow shall rend thee,
        Nor seas shall drown thee.

Thou art whiter than the swan on miry lake,
Thou art whiter than the white gull of the current,
Thou art whiter than the snow of the high
                                    mountains,
Thou art whiter than the love of the angels of
                                    heaven.

Thou art the gracious red rowan
That subdues the ire and anger of all men,
As a sea-wave from flow to ebb,
As a sea-wave from ebb to flow.

The mantle of Christ be placed upon thee,
   To shade thee from thy crown to thy sole;
The mantle of the God of life be keeping thee,
   To be thy champion and thy leader.

Thou shalt not be left in the hand of the wicked,
Thou shalt not be bent in the court of the false;
Thou shalt rise victorious above them
As rise victorious the arches of the waves.

    Thou art the pure love of the clouds,
    Thou art the pure love of the skies,
    Thou art the pure love of the stars,
    Thou art the pure love of the moon,
    Thou art the pure love of the sun,
    Thou art the pure love of the heavens,
    Thou art the pure love of the angels,
    Thou art the pure love of Christ Himself,
    Thou art the pure love of the God of all life.

THE GOSPEL OF THE GOD OF LIFE

The Gospel of the God of life
   To shelter thee, to aid thee;
Yea, the Gospel of beloved Christ
   The holy Gospel of the Lord;

To keep thee from all malice,
   From every dole and dolour;
To keep thee from all spite,
   From evil eye and anguish.

Thou shalt travel thither, thou shalt travel hither,
   Thou shalt travel hill and headland,
Thou shalt travel down, thou shalt travel up,
   Thou shalt travel ocean and narrow.

Christ Himself is shepherd over thee,
   Enfolding thee on every side;
He will not forsake thee hand or foot,
   Nor let evil come anigh thee.

PRAYER FOR TRAVELLING

Life be in my speech,
Sense in what I say,
The bloom of cherries on my lips,
Till I come back again.

The love Christ Jesus gave
Be filling every heart for me,
The love Christ Jesus gave
Filling me for every one.

Traversing corries, traversing forests,
Traversing valleys long and wild.
The fair white Mary still uphold me,
The Shepherd Jesu be my shield,
The fair white Mary still uphold me,
The Shepherd Jesu be my shield.

Work

KINDLING THE FIRE

I will raise the hearth-fire
As Mary would.
The encirclement of Bride and of Mary
On the fire, and on the floor,
And on the household all.

Who are they on the bare floor?
John and Peter and Paul.
Who are they by my bed?
The lovely Bride and her Fosterling.
Who are those watching over my sleep?
The fair loving Mary and her Lamb.
Who is that anear me?
The King of the sun, He himself it is.
Who is that at the back of my head?
The Son of Life without beginning, without time.

SMOORING THE FIRE

I will build the hearth,
As Mary would build it.
The encompassment of Bride and of Mary,
Guarding the hearth, guarding the floor,
Guarding the household all.

Who are they on the lawn without?
Michael the sun-radiant of my trust.
Who are they on the middle of the floor?
John and Peter and Paul.
Who are they by the front of my bed?
Sun-bright Mary and her Son.

The mouth of God ordained,
The angel of God proclaimed,
An angel white in charge of the hearth
Till white day shall come to the embers.
An angel white in charge of the hearth
Till white day shall come to the embers.

MILKING SONG

Come, Mary, and milk my cow,
Come, Bride, and encompass her,
Come, Columba the benign,
　And twine thine arms around my cow.
　　Ho my heifer, ho my gentle heifer,
　　Ho my heifer, ho my gentle heifer,
　　Ho my heifer, ho my gentle heifer,
　　My heifer dear, generous and kind,
　　For the sake of the High King take to thy
　　　　　　　　　　　　　　　calf.

Come, Mary Virgin, to my cow,
Come, great Bride, the beauteous,
Come, thou milkmaid of Jesus Christ,
　And place thine arms beneath my cow.
　　Ho my heifer, ho my gentle heifer.

Lovely black cow, pride of the shieling,
First cow of the byre, choice mother of calves,
Wisps of straw round the cows of the townland,
　A shackle of silk on my heifer beloved.
　　Ho my heifer, ho my gentle heifer.

My black cow, my black cow,
A like sorrow afflicts me and thee,
Thou grieving for thy lovely calf,
　I for my beloved son under the sea,
　　My beloved only son under the sea.

HO, MY HEIFER!

The night the Herdsman was out
No shackle went on a cow,
Lowing ceased not from the mouth of calf
Wailing the Herdsman of the flock,
    Wailing the Herdsman of the flock.

    Ho my heifer! ho my heifer!
    Ho my heifer! my heifer beloved!
    My heartling heart, kind, fond,
    For the sake of the High King take to thy
                                          calf.

The night the Herdsman was missing,
In the Temple He was found.
The King of the moon to come hither!
The King of the sun down from heaven!
    King of the sun down from heaven!

HERDING BLESSING

I will place this flock before me,
As was ordained of the King of the world,
Bride to keep them, to watch them, to tend them,
On ben, on glen, on plain,
  Bride to keep them, to watch them, to tend them,
  On ben, on glen, on plain.

Arise, thou Bride the gentle, the fair,
Take thou thy lint, thy comb, and thy hair,
Since thou to them madest the noble charm,
To keep them from straying, to save them from harm,
  Since thou to them madest the noble charm,
  To keep them from straying, to save them from
                                              harm.

From rocks, from drifts, from streams,
From crooked passes, from destructive pits,
From the straight arrows of the slender ban-shee,
From the heart of envy, from the eye of evil,
  From the straight arrows of the slender ban-
                                              shee,
  From the heart of envy, from the eye of evil.

Mary Mother, tend thou the offspring all,
Bride of the fair palms, guard thou my flocks,
Kindly Columba, thou saint of many powers,
Encompass thou the breeding cows, bestow on me
                                              herds,
  Kindly Columba, thou saint of many powers,
  Encompass thou the breeding cows, bestow on
                                          me herds.

MARKING THE LAMBS

My knife will be new, keen, clean, without stain,
My plaid beneath my knee with my red robe,
I will put sunwise round my breast the first cut
                                    for luck,
The next one after that with the sun as it moves.

A male lamb without blemish, of one colour,
                                    without defect,
Allow thou out on the plain, nor his flowing blood
                                    check,
If the froth remains on the heather with red top,
My flock will be without flaw as long as I change
                                    not the name.

The Three who are above in the City of glory,
Be shepherding my flock and my kine,
Tending them duly in heat, in storm, and in cold,
With the blessing of power driving them down
From yonder height to the sheiling fold.

The name of Ariel of beauteous bloom,
The name of Gabriel herald of the Lamb,
The name of Raphael prince of power,
Surrounding them and saving them.

The name of Muriel and of Mary Virgin,
The name of Peter and of Paul,
The name of James and of John,
Each angel and apostle on their track,
Keeping them alive and their progeny,
        Keeping them alive and their progeny.

BLESSING

This is no second-hand cloth,
And it is not begged,
It is not property of cleric,
It is not property of priest,
And it is not property of pilgrim;

But thine own property,
O son of my body,
By moon and by sun,
In the presence of God,
And keep thou it!

Mayest thou enjoy it,
Mayest thou wear it,
Mayest thou finish it,
Until thou find it
In shreds,
In strips,
In rags,
In tatters!

THE CHANT OF THE WARPING

Thursday of beneficence,
For warping and waulking,
An hundred and fifty strands there shall be
    To number.

Blue thread, very fine,
Two of white by its side,
And scarlet by the side
    Of the madder.

My warp shall be very even,
Give to me Thy blessing, O God,
And to all who are beneath my roof
    In the dwelling.

Michael, thou angel of power,
Mary fair, who art above,
Christ, Thou Shepherd of the people,
Do ye your eternal blessing
    Bestow

On each one who shall lie down,
In name of the Father and of Christ,
And of the Spirit of peacefulness,
    And of grace.

Sprinkle down on us like dew
The gracious wisdom of the mild woman,
Who neglected never the guidance
    Of the High King.

Ward away every evil eye,
And all people of evil wishes,
Consecrate the woof and the warp
    Of every thread.

Place Thou Thine arm around
Each woman who shall be waulking it,
And do Thou aid her in the hour
    Of her need.

Give to me virtues abundant,
As Mary had in her day,
That I may possess the glory
    Of the High King.

Since Thou, O God, it is who givest growth,
To each species and kind,
Give us wool from the surface
    Of the green grass.

Consecrate the flock in every place,
With their little lambs melodious, innocent,
And increase the generations
    Of our herds.

So that we may obtain from them wool,
And nourishing milk to drink,
And that no dearth may be ours
    Of day clothing.

THE CONSECRATION OF THE CLOTH

Well can I say my rune,
Descending with the glen;
    One rune,
    Two runes,
    Three runes,
    Four runes,
    Five runes,
    Six runes.
    Seven runes,
    Seven and a half runes,
    Seven and a half runes.

May the man of this clothing never be wounded,
May torn he never be;
What time he goes into battle or combat,
May the sanctuary shield of the Lord be his.
What time he goes into battle or combat,
May the sanctuary shield of the Lord be his.

This is not second clothing and it is not thigged,
Nor is it the right of sacristan or of priest.

Cresses green culled beneath a stone,
And given to a woman in secret.
The shank of the deer in the head of the herring,
And in the slender tail of the speckled salmon.

CONSECRATION OF THE CLOTH

First consecrator:
> I give the sunwise turn
>> Dependent on the Father.

Second consecrator:
> I give the sunwise turn
>> Dependent on the Son.

Third consecrator:
> I give the sunwise turn
>> Dependent on the Spirit.

The three:
> And each sunwise turn
>> Dependent on the Three,
> And each turn it takes
>> For the sake of the Three.

> And each sunwise turn
>> Dependent on the Three.

HUNTING BLESSING

From my loins begotten wert thou, my son,
May I guide thee the way that is right,
In the holy name of the apostles eleven
In name of the Son of God torn of thee.

In name of James, and Peter, and Paul,
John the baptist, and John the apostle above,
Luke the physician, and Stephen the martyr,
Muriel the fair, and Mary mother of the Lamb.

In name of Patrick holy of the deeds,
And Carmac of the rights and tombs,
Columba beloved, and Adamnan of laws,
Fite calm, and Bride of the milk and kine.

In name of Michael chief of hosts,
In name of Ariel youth of lovely hues,
In name of Uriel of the golden locks,
And Gabriel seer of the Virgin of grace.

The time thou shalt have closed thine eye,
Thou shalt not bend thy knee nor move,
Thou shalt not wound the duck that is swimming,
Never shalt thou harry her of her young.

The white swan of the sweet gurgle,
The speckled dun of the brown tuft,
Thou shalt not cut a feather from their backs,
Till the doom-day, on the crest of the wave.

On the wing be they always
Ere thou place missile to thine ear,
And the fair Mary will give thee of her love,
And the lovely Bride will give thee of her kine.

Thou shalt not eat fallen fish nor fallen flesh,
Nor one bird that thy hand shall not bring down,
Be thou thankful for the one,
Though nine should be swimming.

The fairy swan of Bride of flocks,
The fairy duck of Mary of peace.

CONSECRATING THE CHASE

In name of the Holy Three-fold as one,
In word, in deed, and in thought,
I am bathing mine own hands,
In the light and in the elements of the sky.

Vowing that I shall never return in my life,
Without fishing, without fowling either,
Without game, without venison down from the
                                              hill,
Without fat, without blubber from out the copse.

O Mary tender-fair, gentle-fair, loving-fair,
Avoid thou to me the silvery salmon dead on the
                                          salt sea,
A duck with her brood an it please thee to show
                                               me,
A nest by the edge of the water where it does not
                                               dry.

The grey-hen on the crown of the knoll,
The black-cock of the hoarse croon,
After the strength of the sun has gone down,
Avoid, oh, avoid thou to me the hearing of them.

O Mary, fragrant mother of my King,
Crown thou me with the crown of thy peace,
Place thine own regal robe of gold to protect me,
And save me with the saving of Christ,
        Save me with the saving of Christ.

CHOICE OF TIMBER

Choose the willow of the streams,
   Choose the hazel of the rocks,
Choose the alder of the marshes,
   Choose the birch of the waterfalls.

Choose the ash of the shade,
   Choose the yew of resilience,
Choose the elm of the brae,
   Choose the oak of the sun.

CHOICE

These are said to be the best.

Boat of board-ends,
   Shoe of welt-ends,
Stack of ear-ends,
   Creel of rod-ends.

FISHING BLESSING

The day of light has come upon us,
Christ is born of the Virgin.

In His name I sprinkle the water
Upon every thing within my court.

Thou King of deeds and powers above,
Thy fishing blessing pour down on us.

I will sit me down with an oar in my grasp,
I will row me seven hundred and seven strokes.

I will cast down my hook,
The first fish which I bring up

In the name of Christ, King of the elements,
The poor shall have it at his wish.

And the king of fishers, the brave Peter,
He will after it give me his blessing.

Ariel, Gabriel, and John,
Raphael benign, and Paul,

Columba, tender in every distress,
And Mary fair, the endowed of grace.

Encompass ye us to the fishing-bank of ocean,
And still ye to us the crest of the waves.

Be the King of kings at the end of our course,
Of lengthened life and of lasting happiness.

Be the crown of the King from the Three on high,
Be the cross of Christ adown to shield us,
    The crown of the King from the Three above,
    The cross of Christ adown to shield us.

THE OCEAN BLESSING

O Thou who pervadest the heights,
Imprint on us Thy gracious blessing,
Carry us over the surface of the sea,
Carry us safely to a haven of peace,
Bless our boatmen and our boat,
Bless our anchors and our oars,
Each stay and halyard and traveller,
Our mainsails to our tall masts
Keep, O King of the elements, in their place
That we may return home in peace;
I myself will sit down at the helm,
It is God's own Son who will give me guidance,
As He gave to Columba the mild
What time he set stay to sails.

Mary, Bride, Michael, Paul,
Peter, Gabriel, John of love,
Pour ye down from above the dew
That would make our faith to grow,
Establish ye us in the Rock of rocks,
In every law that love exhibits,
That we may reach the land of glory,
Where peace and love and mercy reign,
All vouchsafed to us through grace;
Never shall the canker worm get near us,
We shall there be safe for ever,
We shall not be in the bonds of death
Though we are of the seed of Adam.

On the Feast Day of Michael, the Feast Day of
                                    Martin,
The Feast Day of Andrew, band of mercy,
The Feast Day of Bride, day of my choice,
Cast ye the serpent into the ocean,
So that the sea may swallow her up;
On the Feast Day of Patrick, day of power,
Reveal to us the storm from the north,
Quell its wrath and blunt its fury,
Lessen its fierceness, kill its cold.

On the Day of the Three Kings on high,
Subdue to us the crest of the waves,
On Beltane Day give us the dew,
On John's Day the gentle wind,
The Day of Mary the great of fame,
Ward off us the storm from the west;
Each day and night, storm and calm,
Be Thou with us, O Chief of chiefs,
Be Thou Thyself to us a compass-chart,
Be Thine hand on the helm of our rudder,
Thine own hand, Thou God of the elements,
Early and late as is becoming,
        Early and late as is becoming.

OCEAN BLESSING

God the Father all-powerful, benign,
Jesu the Son of tears and of sorrow,
With thy co-assistance, O! Holy Spirit.

The Three-One, ever-living, ever-mighty,
                                    everlasting,
Who brought the Children of Israel through the
                                    Red Sea,
And Jonah to land from the belly of the great
                        creature of the ocean,

Who brought Paul and his companions in the ship,
From the torment of the sea, from the dolour of
                                    the waves,
From the gale that was great, from the storm that
                                    was heavy.

When the storm poured on the Sea of Galilee,
        *   *   *   *   *   *
        *   *   *   *   *   *

Sain us and shield and sanctify us,
Be Thou, King of the elements, seated at our helm,
And lead us in peace to the end of our journey.

With winds mild, kindly, benign, pleasant,
Without swirl, without whirl, without eddy,
That would do no harmful deed to us.

We ask all things of Thee, O God,
According to Thine own will and word.

Charms and Banishings

CHARM FOR FEAR BY NIGHT

God before me, God behind me,
God above me, God below me;
I on the path of God,
God upon my track.

    Who is there on land?
    Who is there on wave?
    Who is there on billow?
    Who is there by door-post?
    Who is along with us?
      God and Lord.

I am here abroad,
I am here in need,
I am here in pain,
I am here in straits,
I am here alone,
    O God, aid me.

GOD OF THE MOON, GOD OF THE SUN

God of the moon, God of the sun,
Who ordained to us the Son of mercy.
The fair Mary upon her knee,
Christ the King of life in her lap.
I am the cleric established,
Going round the founded stones,
I behold mansions, I behold shores,
I behold angels floating,
I behold the shapely rounded column
Coming landwards in friendship to us.

THWARTING THE EYE

Twelve eyes against every malice,
Twelve eyes against every envy,
Twelve eyes against every purpose,
Twelve eyes against every hope,
Twelve eyes against every intent,
Twelve eyes against every eye,
The twelve eyes of the Son of the God of life,
    The twelve eyes of the Son of the God of life.

EXORCISM OF THE EYE

I trample upon the eye,
As tramples the duck upon the lake,
As tramples the swan upon the water,
As tramples the horse upon the plain,
As tramples the cow upon the nook,
As tramples the host of the elements,
    As tramples the host of the elements.

Power of wind I have over it,
Power of wrath I have over it,
Power of fire I have over it,
Power of thunder I have over it,
Power of lightning I have over it,
Power of storms I have over it,
Power of moon I have over it,
Power of sun I have over it,
Power of stars I have over it,
Power of firmament I have over it,
Power of the heavens
And of the worlds I have over it,
    Power of the heavens
    And of the worlds I have over it.

A portion of it upon the grey stones,
A portion of it upon the steep hills,
A portion of it upon the fast falls,

A portion of it upon the fair meads,
And a portion upon the great salt sea,
She herself is the best instrument to carry it,
    The great salt sea,
    The best instrument to carry it.

In name of the Three of Life,
In name of the Sacred Three,
In name of all the Secret Ones,
And of the Powers together.

SPELL OF THE EYE

The spell the great white Mary sent
To Bride the lovely fair,
For sea, for land, for water, and for withering
glance,
For teeth of wolf, for testicle of wolf.

Whoso laid on thee the eye,
May it oppress himself,
May it oppress his house,
May it oppress his flocks.

Let me subdue the eye,
Let me avert the eye,
The three complete tongues of fullness,
In the arteries of the heart,
In the vitals of the navel.

From the bosom of Father,
From the bosom of Son,
From the bosom of Holy Spirit.

CHARM AGAINST VENOM

Be the eye of God betwixt me and each eye,
The purpose of God betwixt me and each purpose,
The hand of God betwixt me and each hand,
The shield of God betwixt me and each shield,
The desire of God betwixt me and each desire,
The bridle of God betwixt me and each bridle,
    And no mouth can curse me.

Be the pain of Christ betwixt me and each pain,
The love of Christ betwixt me and each love,
The dearness of Christ betwixt me and each
                            dearness,
The kindness of Christ betwixt me and each
                            kindness,
The wish of Christ betwixt me and each wish,
The will of Christ betwixt me and each will,
    And no venom can wound me.

Be the might of Christ betwixt me and each might,
The right of Christ betwixt me and each right,
The flowing of Spirit betwixt me and each flowing,
The laving of Spirit betwixt me and each laving,
The bathing of Spirit betwixt me and each
                            bathing,
    And no ill thing can touch me.

CHARM AGAINST WOMEN

O Lord and God of life,
  Ward off from me the bane of the silent women.

O Father and God of life,
  Ward off from me the bane of the wanton
                                    women.

  O Father everlasting and God of life,
  Ward off from me the bane of the fairy women.

O Father everlasting and God of life,
  Ward off from me the bane of the false women.

O Father everlasting and God of life,
  Crown Thou me with the crown of Thy love.

PRAYER

Each day be glad to thee,
No day be sad to thee,
  Life rich and satisfying.

Plenty be on thy course,
A son be on thy coming,
  A daughter on thine arriving.

The strong help of the serpent be thine,
The strong help of fire be thine,
  The strong help of the graces.

The love-death of joy be thine,
The love-death of Mary be thine,
  The loving arm of thy Saviour.

GOOD WISH

Wisdom of serpent be thine,
Wisdom of raven be thine,
   Wisdom of valiant eagle.

Voice of swan be thine,
Voice of honey be thine,
   Voice of the son of the stars.

Bounty of sea be thine,
Bounty of land be thine,
   Bounty of the Father of heaven.

THE YARROW

I will pluck the yarrow fair,
That more benign shall be my face,
That more warm shall be my lips,
That more chaste shall be my speech,
Be my speech the beams of the sun,
Be my lips the sap of the strawberry.

May I be an isle in the sea,
May I be a hill on the shore,
May I be a star in waning of the moon,
May I be a staff to the weak,
Wound can I every man,
Wound can no man me.

THE YARROW

I will pluck the yarrow fair,
That more brave shall be my hand,
That more warm shall be my lips,
That more swift shall be my foot;
May I an island be at sea,
May I a rock be on land,
That I can afflict any man,
    No man can afflict me.

THE ASPEN

Malison be on thee, O aspen tree!
  On thee was crucified the King of the
                               mountains,
In whom were driven the nails without clench,
  And that driving crucifying was exceeding
                                 sore —
  That driving crucifying was exceeding sore.

Malison be on thee, O aspen hard!
  On thee was crucified the King of glory,
Sacrifice of Truth, Lamb without blemish,
  His blood in streams down pouring —
  His blood in streams down pouring.

Malison be on thee, O aspen cursed!
  On thee was crucified the King of kings,
And malison be on the eye that seeth thee,
  If it maledict thee not, thou aspen cursed —
  If it maledict thee not, thou aspen cursed!

SILVERWEED

Honey under ground
Silverweed of spring.
Honey and condiment
Whisked whey of summer.
Honey and fruitage
Carrot of autumn.
Honey and crunching
Nuts of winter
Between Feast of Andrew
  And Christmastide.

THE CHARM OF THE FIGWORT

I will cull the figwort,
Of thousand blessings, of thousand virtues,
The calm Bride endowing it to me,
The fair Mary enriching it to me,
The great Mary, aid-Mother of the people.

Came the nine joys,
With the nine waves,
To cull the figwort,
Of thousand blessings, of thousand virtues —
Of thousand blessings, of thousand virtues.

The arm of Christ about me,
The face of Christ before me,
The shade of Christ over me,
My noble plant is being culled —
My noble plant is being culled.

In name of the Father of wisdom,
In name of the Christ of Pasch,
In name of the Spirit of grace,
Who in the struggles of my death,
Will not leave me till Doom —
    Who in the struggles of my death,
    Will not leave me till Doom.

ST COLUMBA'S PLANT

I will pluck what I meet,
As in communion with my saint,
To stop the wiles of wily men,
    And the arts of foolish women.

I will pluck my Columba plant,
As a prayer to my King,
That mine be the power of Columba's plant,
    Over every one I see.

I will pluck the leaf above,
As ordained of the High King,
In name of the Three of glory,
    And of Mary, Mother of Christ.

THE SHAMROCK OF POWER

Thou shamrock of foliage,
Thou shamrock of power,
Thou shamrock of foliage,
Which Mary had under the bank,
Thou shamrock of my love,
Of most beauteous hue,
I would choose thee in death,
To grow on my grave,
    I would choose thee in death,
    To grow on my grave.

Encompassing

ENCOMPASSING

The compassing of God be on thee,
   The compassing of the God of life.

The compassing of Christ be on thee,
   The compassing of the Christ of love.

The compassing of Spirit be on thee,
   The compassing of the Spirit of Grace.

The compassing of the Three be on thee,
   The compassing of the Three preserve thee,
   The compassing of the Three preserve thee.

THE THREE

The Three Who are over me,
The Three Who are below me,
The Three Who are above me here,
The Three Who are above me yonder;
The Three Who are in the earth,
The Three Who are in the air,
The Three Who are in the heaven,
    The Three Who are in the great pouring sea.

ENCOMPASSING

The compassing of God and His right hand
Be upon my form and upon my frame;
The compassing of the High King and the grace
                                of the Trinity
Be upon me abiding ever eternally,
  Be upon me abiding ever eternally.

May the compassing of the Three shield me in my
                                    means,
The compassing of the Three shield me this day,
The compassing of the Three shield me this night
From hate, from harm, from act, from ill,
  From hate, from harm, from act, from ill.

ENCOMPASSMENT

The holy Apostles' guarding,
The gentle martyrs' guarding,
The nine angels' guarding,
    Be cherishing me, be aiding me.

The quiet Brigit's guarding,
The gentle Mary's guarding,
The warrior Michael's guarding,
    Be shielding me, be aiding me.

The God of the elements' guarding,
The loving Christ's guarding,
The Holy Spirit's guarding,
    Be cherishing me, be aiding me.

GRACE

Grace of love be thine,
Grace of floor be thine,
Grace of castle be thine,
Grace of court be thine,
   Grace and pride of homeland be thine.

The guard of the God of life be thine,
The guard of the loving Christ be thine,
The guard of the Holy Spirit be thine,

To cherish thee,
To aid thee,
To enfold thee.

The Three be about thy head,
The Three be about thy breast,
The Three be about thy body
   Each night and each day,
In the encompassment of the Three
   Throughout thy life long.

PRAYER OF PROTECTION

Thou Michael of militance,
  Thou Michael of wounding,
Shield me from the grudge
  Of ill-wishers this night,
  Ill-wishers this night.

Thou Brigit of the kine,
  Thou Brigit of the mantles,
Shield me from the ban
  Of the fairies of the knolls,
  The fairies of the knolls.

Thou Mary of mildness,
  Thou Mary of honour,
Succour me and shield me
  With thy linen mantle,
  With thy linen mantle.

Thou Christ of the tree,
  Thou Christ of the cross,
Snatch me from the snares
  Of the spiteful ones of evil,
  The spiteful ones of evil.

Thou Father of the waifs,
  Thou Father of the naked,
Draw me to the shelter-house
  Of the Saviour of the poor,
  The Saviour of the poor.

JESUS THE ENCOMPASSER

Jesu! Only-begotten Son and Lamb of God the
                               Father,
Thou didst give the wine-blood of Thy body to
                        buy me from the grave.
My Christ! my Christ! my shield, my encircler,
Each day, each night, each light, each dark;
  My Christ! my Christ! my shield, my encircler,
  Each day, each night, each light, each dark.

Be near me, uphold me, my treasure, my triumph,

In my lying, in my standing, in my watching, in
  my sleeping.

Jesu, Son of Mary! my helper, my encircler,
Jesu, Son of David! my strength everlasting;
  Jesu, Son of Mary! my helper, my encircler,
  Jesu, Son of David! my strength everlasting.

THE PILGRIMS' SAFEGUARDING

I am placing my soul and my body
Under thy guarding this night, O Brigit,
O calm Fostermother of the Christ without sin,
O calm Fostermother of the Christ of wounds.

I am placing my soul and my body
Under thy guarding this night, O Mary,
O tender Mother of the Christ of the poor,
O tender Mother of the Christ of tears.

I am placing my soul and my body
Under Thy guarding this night, O Christ,
O Thou Son of the tears, of the wounds, of the
                                        piercings,
May Thy cross this night be shielding me.

I am placing my soul and my body
Under Thy guarding this night, O God,
O Thou Father of help to the poor feeble pilgrims,
Protector of earth and of heaven,
        Protector of earth and of heaven.

THOU, MY SOUL'S HEALER

Thou, my soul's Healer,
Keep me at even,
Keep me at morning,
Keep me at noon,
On rough course faring,
Help and safeguard
My means this night.
   I am tired, astray, and stumbling,
   Shield Thou me from snare and sin.

Prayers and Blessings

HOLY FATHER OF GLORY

Thanks be to Thee, Holy Father of Glory,
Father kind, ever-loving, ever-powerful,
Because of all the abundance, favour, and
                                        deliverance
That Thou bestowest upon us in our need.
Whatever providence befalls us as thy children,
In our portion, in our lot, in our path,
Give to us with it the rich gifts of Thine hand
And the joyous blessing of Thy mouth.

We are guilty and polluted, O God,
In spirit, in heart, and in flesh,
In thought, in word, in act,
We are hard in Thy sight in sin.
Put Thou forth to us the power of Thy love,
Be thou leaping over the mountains of our
                                        transgressions,
And wash us in the true blood of conciliation,
Like the down of the mountain, like the lily of the
                                        lake.

In the steep common path of our calling,
Be it easy or uneasy to our flesh,
Be it bright or dark for us to follow,
Thine own perfect guidance be upon us.
Be Thou a shield to us from the wiles of the
                                        deceiver,
From the arch-destroyer with his arrows pursuing
                                        us,
And in each secret thought our minds get to weave,
Be Thou Thyself on our helm and at our sheet.

THE THREE

In name of Father,
In name of Son,
In name of Spirit,
  Three in One:

Father cherish me,
Son cherish me,
Spirit cherish me,
  Three all-kindly.

God make me holy,
Christ make me holy,
Spirit make me holy,
  Three all-holy.

Three aid my hope,
Three aid my love,
Three aid mine eye,
  And my knee from stumbling,
  My knee from stumbling.

PRAYER

Relieve Thou, O God, each one
In suffering on land or sea,
In grief or wounded or weeping,
And lead them to the house of Thy peace
    This night.

I am weary, weak and cold,
I am weary of travelling land and sea,
I am weary of traversing moorland and billow,
Grant me peace in the nearness of Thy repose
    This night.

  Beloved Father of my God,
  Accept the caring for my tears;
  I would wish reconcilement with Thee,
  Through the witness and the ransom
     Of Thy Son;

  To be resting with Jesus
  In the dwelling of peace,
  In the paradise of gentleness,
  In the fairy-bower
    Of mercy.

A PRAYER FOR GRACE

I am bending my knee
In the eye of the Father who created me,
In the eye of the Son who died for me,
In the eye of the Spirit who cleansed me,
 In love and desire.

Pour down upon us from heaven
The rich blessing of Thy forgiveness;
Thou who art uppermost in the City,
 Be Thou patient with us.

Grant to us, Thou Saviour of Glory,
The fear of God, the love of God, and His
          affection,
And the will of God to do on earth at all times
As angels and saints do in heaven;
Each day and night give us Thy peace.
 Each day and night give us Thy peace.

INVOCATION FOR JUSTICE

God, I am bathing my face
In the nine rays of the sun,
As Mary bathed her Son
    In generous milk fermented.

Sweetness be in my face,
Riches be in my countenance,
Comb-honey be in my tongue,
    My breath as the incense.

Black is yonder house,
Blacker men therein;
I am the white swan,
    Queen over them.

I will go in the name of God,
In likeness of deer, in likeness of horse,
In likeness of serpent, in likeness of king,
    More victorious am I than all persons.

A RESTING PRAYER

God shield the house, the fire, the kine,
Every one who dwells herein to-night.
Shield myself and my beloved group,
Preserve us from violence and from harm;
Preserve us from foes this night,
For the sake of the Son of the Mary Mother,
In this place, and in every place wherein they
                                dwell to-night,
On this night and on every night,
    This night and every night.

HOUSE PROTECTING

God, bless the world and all that is therein.
God, bless my spouse and my children,
God, bless the eye that is in my head,
And bless, O God, the handling of my hand;
What time I rise in the morning early,
What time I lie down late in bed,
    Bless my rising in the morning early,
    And my lying down late in bed.

God, protect the house, and the household,
God, consecrate the children of the motherhood,
God, encompass the flocks and the young;
Be Thou after them and tending them,
What time the flocks ascend hill and wold,
What time I lie down to sleep,
    What time the flocks ascend hill and wold,
    What time I lie down in peace to sleep.

THE MEAL

Give us, O God, of the morning meal,
    Benefit to the body, the frame of the soul;
Give us, O God, of the seventh bread,
    Enough for our need at evening close.

Give us, O God, of the honey-sweet foaming milk,
    The sap and milk of the fragrant farms,
And give us, O God, along with Thy sleep,
    Rest in the shade of Thy covenant Rock.

Give us this night of the corn that shall last,
    Give us this night of the drink that shall hurt
                                     not;
Give us this night, anear to the heavens,
    The chalice of Mary mild, the tender.

Be with us by day, be with us by night,
    Be with us by light and by dark,
In our lying down and in our rising up,
    In speech, in walk, in prayer.

PRAYER OF DISTRESS

May the cross of the crucifixion tree
    Upon the wounded back of Christ
Deliver me from distress,
    From death and from spells.

The cross of Christ without fault,
    All outstretched towards me;
O God, bless to me my lot
    Before my going out.

What harm soever may be therein
    May I not take thence,
For the sake of Christ the guileless,
    For the sake of the King of power.

In name of the King of life,
In name of the Christ of love,
In name of the Holy Spirit,
    The Triune of my strength.

BLESSINGS

May God's goodness be yours,
  And well and seven times well
May you spend your lives.

The love of your creator be with you.

The eye of the great God be upon you,
The eye of the God of glory be on you,
The eye of the Son of Mary Virgin be on you,
The eye of the Spirit mild be on you,
  To aid you and to shepherd you;
Oh the kindly eye of the Three be on you,
  To aid you and to shepherd you.

The compassing of the saints be upon you,
The compassing of the angels be upon you;
  Oh the compassing of all the saints
  And of the nine angels be upon you.

Be the eye of God dwelling with you,
The foot of Christ in guidance with you,
The shower of the Spirit pouring on you,
    Richly and generously.

The compassing of the King of life be yours,
The compassing of loving Christ be yours,
The compassing of Holy Spirit be yours
    Unto the crown of the life eternal,
    Unto the crown of the life eternal.

My own blessing be with you,
The blessing of God be with you,
The blessing of Spirit be with you
    And with your children,
        With you and with your children.

The love and affection of the angels be to you,
The love and affection of the saints be to you,
The love and affection of heaven be to you,
    To guard you and to cherish you.

May the everlasting Father shield you
East and west wherever you go.

May God make safe to you each steep,
May God make open to you each pass,
May God make clear to you each road,
　And may He take you in the clasp of His own
　　　　　　　　　　　　　　　two hands.

May the Father take you
　In His fragrant clasp of love,
When you go across the flooding streams
And the black river of death.

May the King shield you in the valleys,
May Christ aid you on the mountains,
May Spirit bathe you on the slopes,
　In hollow, on hill, on plain,
　Mountain, valley and plain.

The shape of Christ be towards me,
The shape of Christ be to me,
The shape of Christ be before me,
The shape of Christ be behind me,
The shape of Christ be over me,
The shape of Christ be under me,
The shape of Christ be with me,
The shape of Christ be around me
On Monday and on Sunday;
    The shape of Christ be around me
    On Monday and on Sunday.

The peace of God be with you,
The peace of Christ be with you,
The peace of Spirit be with you
    And with your children,
From the day that we have here to-day
    To the day of the end of your lives,
    Until the day of the end of your lives.

Festivals and Saints

THE FIRST MIRACLE OF CHRIST

Joseph and Mary went
To the numbering up,
And the birds began chorusing
In the woods of the turtle-doves.

The two were walking the way,
Till they reached a thick wood,
And in the wood there was fruit
Which was as red as the rasp.

That was the time when she was great,
That she was carrying the King of grace,
And she took a desire for the fruit
That was growing on the gracious slope.

Then spoke Mary to Joseph,
In a voice low and sweet,
'Give to me of the fruit, Joseph,
That I may quench my desire.'

And Joseph spoke to Mary,
And the hard pain in his breast,
'I will give thee of the fruit, Mary,
But who is the father of thy burthen?'

Then it was that the Babe spoke,
From out of her womb,
'Bend ye down every beautiful bough,
That my Mother may quench her desire.'

And from the bough that was highest,
To the bough that was lowest,
They all bent down to her knee,
And Mary partook of the fruit
In her loved land of prophecy.

Then Joseph said to Mary,
And he full of heavy contrition,
'It is carrying Him thou art,
The King of glory and of grace.
Blessed art thou, Mary,
     Among the women of all lands.
Blessed art thou, Mary,
     Among the women of all lands.'

CHRISTMAS CAROL

This night is the long night,
    Hù ri vì hó hù,
It will snow and it will drift,
    Hù ri vì hó hù,
White snow there will be till day,
    Hù ri vì hó hù,
White moon there will be till morn,
    Hù ri vì hó hù.
This night is the eve of the Great Nativity,
    Hù ri vì hó hù,
This night is born Mary Virgin's Son,
    Hù ri vì hó hù,
This night is born Jesus, Son of the King of glory,
    Hù ri vì hó hù,
This night is born to us the root of our joy,
    Hù ri vì hó hù,
This night gleamed the sun of the mountains high,
    Hù ri vì hó hù,
This night gleamed sea and shore together,
    Hù ri vì hó hù,
This night was born Christ the King of greatness,
    Hù ri vì hó hù,
Ere it was heard that the Glory was come,
    Hù ri vì hó hù,
Heard was the wave upon the strand,
    Hù ri vì hó hù;
Ere 'twas heard that His foot had reached the
                           earth,
    Hù ri vì hó hù,

Heard was the song of the angels glorious,
  Hù ri vì hó hù.
This night is the long night,
  Hù ri vì hó hù.

Glowed to Him wood and tree,
  Glowed to Him mount and sea,
Glowed to Him land and plain,
  When that His foot was come to earth.

THE CHILD OF GLORY

The Child of glory
The Child of Mary,
Born in the stable
    The King of all,
Who came to the wilderness
And in our stead suffered;
Happy they are counted
    Who to Him are near.

When He Himself saw
That we were in travail,
Heaven opened graciously
    Over our head:
We beheld Christ,
The Spirit of truth,
The same drew us in
    'Neath the shield of His crown.

Strengthen our hope,
Enliven our joyance,
Keep us valiant,
    Faithful and near,
O light of our lantern,
Along with the virgins,
Singing in glory
    The anthem new.

CHRISTMAS CHANT

Hail King! hail King! blessed is He! blessed is He!
Hail King! hail King! blessed is He! blessed is He!
      Ho, hail! blessed the King!
      Ho, hi! let there be joy!

Prosperity be upon this dwelling,
On all that ye have heard and seen,
On the bare bright floor flags,
On the shapely standing stone staves,
      Hail King! hail King! blessed is He! blessed
                         is He!

Bless this house and all that it contains,
From rafter and stone and beam;
Deliver it to God from pall to cover,
Be the healing of men therein,
      Hail King! hail King! blessed is He! blessed
                         is He!

Be ye in lasting possession of the house,
Be ye healthy about the hearth,
Many be the ties and stakes in the homestead,
People dwelling on this foundation,
      Hail King! hail King! blessed is He! blessed
                         is He!

Offer to the Being from found to cover,
Include stave and stone and beam;
Offer again both rods and cloth,
Be health to the people therein,
    Hail King! hail King! blessed is He! blessed
                                       is He!
    Hail King! hail King! blessed is He! blessed
                                       is He!

        Ho, hail! blessed the King!
          Let there be joy!

        Blessed the King,
        Without beginning, without ending,
        To everlasting, to eternity,
            Every generation for aye,
            Ho! hi! let there be joy!

THE BLESSING OF THE NEW YEAR

God, bless to me the new day,
Never vouchsafed to me before;
It is to bless Thine own presence
Thou hast given me this time, O God.

Bless Thou to me mine eye,
May mine eye bless all it sees;
I will bless my neighbour,
May my neighbour bless me.

God, give me a clean heart,
Let me not from sight of Thine eye;
Bless to me my children and my wife,
And bless to me my means and my cattle.

GOD OF THE MOON

God of the moon, God of the sun,
God of the globe, God of the stars,
God of the waters, the land, and the skies,
Who ordained to us the King of promise.

It was Mary fair who went upon her knee,
It was the King of life who went upon her lap,
Darkness and tears were set behind,
And the star of guidance went up early.

Illumed the land, illumed the world,
Illumed doldrum and current,
Grief was laid and joy was raised,
Music was set up with harp and pedal-harp.

SAINT BRIGIT

Brigit of the mantles,
　　Brigit of the peat-heap,
Bright of the twining hair,
　　Brigit of the augury.

Brigit of the white feet,
　　Brigit of calmness,
Brigit of the white palms,
　　Brigit of the kine.

Brigit, woman-comrade,
　　Brigit of the peat-heap,
Brigit, woman-helper,
　　Brigit, woman mild.

Brigit, own tress of Mary,
　　Brigit, Nurse of Christ, —
Each day and each night
　　That I say the Descent of Brigit,

　　　I shall not be slain,
　　　　I shall not be wounded,
　　　I shall not be put in cell,
　　　　I shall not be gashed,
　　　I shall not be torn in sunder,
　　　　I shall not be despoiled,

I shall not be down-trodden,
  I shall not be made naked,
I shall not be rent,
Nor will Christ
  Leave me forgotten.

Nor sun shall burn me,
Nor fire shall burn me,
Nor beam shall burn me,
Nor moon shall burn me.

Nor river shall drown me,
Nor brine shall drown me,
Nor flood shall drown me,
Nor water shall drown me.

Nightmare shall not lie on me
  Black-sheep shall not lie on
Spell-sleep shall not lie on me.
  'Luaths-luis' shall not lie on

I am under the keeping
Of my Saint Mary;
My companion beloved
  Is Brigit.

THE BELTANE BLESSING

Mary, thou mother of saints,
Bless our flocks and bearing kine;
Hate nor scath let not come near us,
Drive from us the ways of the wicked.

Keep thine eye every Monday and Tuesday
On the bearing kine and the pairing queys;
Accompany us from hill to sea,
Gather thyself the sheep and their progeny.

Every Wednesday and Thursday be with them,
Be thy gracious hand always about them;
Tend the cows down to their stalls,
Tend the sheep down to their folds!

Every Friday be thou, O Saint, at their head,
Lead the sheep from the face of the bens,
With their innocent little lambs following them,
Encompass them with God's encompassing.

Every Saturday be likewise with them,
Bring the goats in with their young,
Every kid and goat to the sea side,
And from the Rock of Aegir on high,
With cresses green about its summit.

The strength of the Triune be our shield in
                                             distress,
The strength of Christ, His peace and His Pasch,
The strength of the Spirit, Physician of health,
And of the precious Father, the King of grace.

    *   *   *   *   *

And of every other saint who succeeded them
And who earned the repose of the kingdom of
                                             God.

Bless ourselves and our children,
Bless every one who shall come from our loins,
Bless him whose name we bear,
Bless, O God, her from whose womb we came.

Every holiness, blessing and power,
Be yielded to us every time and every hour,
In name of the Holy Threefold above,
Father, Son, and Spirit everlasting.

Be the Cross of Christ to shield us downward,
Be the Cross of Christ to shield us upward,
Be the Cross of Christ to shield us roundward,
Accepting our Beltane blessing from us,
    Accepting our Beltane blessing from us.

MICHAEL OF THE ANGELS

O Michael of the angels
And the righteous in heaven,
Shield thou my soul
  With the shade of thy wing;
Shield thou my soul
  On earth and in heaven;

From foes upon earth,
From foes beneath earth,
From foes in concealment
Protect and encircle
  My soul 'neath thy wing,
    Oh my soul with the shade of thy wing!

TO WHOM SHALL I OFFER OBLATION?

To whom shall I offer oblation
In name of Michael on high?
I will give tithe of my means
To the forsaken illustrious One.

Because of all that I have seen,
Of His peace and of His mercy,
Lift Thou my soul to Thee, O Son of God,
Nor leave me ever.

Remember me in the mountain,
Under Thy wing shield Thou me;
Rock of truth, do not forsake me,
My wish it were ever to be near Thee.

Give to me the wedding garment,
Be angels conversing with me in every need,
Be the holy apostles protecting me,
The fair Mary and Thou, Jesu of grace,
    The fair Mary and Thou, Jesu of grace.

SOUL PEACE

Since Thou Christ it was who didst buy the soul —
At the time of yielding the life,
At the time of pouring the sweat,
At the time of offering the clay,
At the time of shedding the blood,
At the time of balancing the beam,
At the time of severing the breath,
At the time of delivering the judgment,
Be its peace upon Thine own ingathering;
Jesus Christ Son of gentle Mary,
Be its peace upon Thine own ingathering,
    O Jesus! upon Thine own ingathering.

And may Michael white kindly,
High king of the holy angels,
Take possession of the beloved soul,
And shield it home to the Three of surpassing
                                            love,
    Oh! to the Three of surpassing love.

BRIAN

(Brian was the name of Michael's steed, famed for its
swiftness and whiteness.)

    Michael's Brian was
        As white as the snow of the peaks,
        As white as the foam of the waves,
        As white as the cotton of the meads,
        And nearly as white as the angel
                                  victorious.

    Michael's Brian was
        As swift as the swift of the spring,
        As swift as the wind of March,
        As swift as the deadly levin,
        And nearly as swift as the shaft of death.

Moon

MOON WORSHIP

Glory to thee for ever,
    Thou bright moon, this night;
Thyself art ever
    The glorious lamp of the poor.

THE NEW MOON

Hail to thee, thou new moon,
   Guiding jewel of gentleness!
I am bending to thee my knee,
   I am offering thee my love.

I am bending to thee my knee,
   I am giving thee my hand,
I am lifting to thee mine eye,
   O new moon of the seasons.

Hail to thee, thou new moon,
   Joyful maiden of my love!
Hail to thee, thou new moon,
   Joyful maiden of the graces!

Thou art travelling in thy course,
   Thou art steering the full tides;
Thou art illuming to us thy face,
   O new moon of the seasons.

Thou queen-maiden of guidance,
   Thou queen-maiden of good fortune,
Thou queen-maiden my beloved,
   Thou new moon of the seasons!

QUEEN OF THE NIGHT

Hail unto thee,
  Jewel of the night!

Beauty of the heavens,
  Jewel of the night!

Mother of the stars,
  Jewel of the night!

Fosterling of the sun,
  Jewel of the night!

Majesty of the stars,
  Jewel of the night!

BEAUTEOUS FAIR ONE OF GRACE

Hail to thee, thou new moon
   Beauteous guidant of the sky;
Hail to thee, thou new moon,
   Beauteous fair one of grace.

Hail to thee, thou new moon,
   Beauteous guidant of the stars;
Hail to thee, thou new moon,
   Beauteous loved one of my heart.

Hail to thee, thou new moon,
   Beauteous guidant of the clouds;
Hail to thee, thou new moon,
   Beauteous dear one of the heavens!

NEW MOON

There, see, the new moon,
  The King of life blessing her;
Fragrant be every night
  Whereon she shall shine!

Be her lustre full
  To each one in need;
Be her course complete
  To each one beset.

Be her light above
  With every one in straits;
Be her guidance below
  With every one in need.

May the moon of moons
  Be coming through thick clouds
On me and on every one
  Coming through dark tears.

May God's hand on me dwell
  In every strait that me befalls,
Now and till the hour of my death,
  And till the day of my resurrection.

THE NEW MOON

In name of the Holy Spirit of grace,
In name of the Father of the City of peace,
In name of Jesus who took death off us,
Oh! in name of the Three who shield us in every
need,
If well thou hast found us to-night,
Seven times better mayest thou leave us without
harm,
Thou bright white Moon of the seasons,
Bright white Moon of the seasons.

Mary

A PRAYER

O God,
In my deeds,
In my words,
In my wishes,
In my reason,
And in the fulfilling of my desires,
In my sleep,
In my dreams,
In my repose,
In my thoughts,
In my heart and soul always,
May the blessed Virgin Mary,
And the promised Branch of Glory dwell,
    Oh! in my heart and soul always,
    May the blessed Virgin Mary,
    And the fragrant Branch of Glory dwell.

PRAYER TO MARY MOTHER

O Mary Maiden,
　　Never was known
One who was placed
　　'Neath thy generous care,

Who asked thy mercy,
　　Who asked thy shielding,
Who asked thy succour
　　With truthful heart,

Who found not thy solace,
　　Who found not thy peace,
Who found not the succour
　　For which he sought.

That gives unto me
　　The hope excelling
That my tears and my prayer
　　May find guest-room with thee.

My heart is content
　　To kneel at thy footstool,
My heart is content
　　In thy favour and hearing;

To come into thy presence,
　　Beauteous one of smiles,
To come into thy presence,
　　Beauteous one of women;

To come into thy presence,
  Queen-maiden of mankind,
To come into thy presence,
  Queen-maiden of the worlds;

To come into thy presence,
  O flower-garland of branches,
To come into thy presence,
  Bright garland of the heavens;

To come into thy presence,
  O Mother of the Lamb of Grace,
To come into thy presence,
  O Mother of the Paschal Lamb;

To come into thy presence,
  O river of seed,
To come into thy presence,
  O vessel of peace;

To come into thy presence,
  O fountain of healing,
To come into thy presence,
  O well-spring of grace;

To come into thy presence,
  Thou dwelling of meekness,
To come into thy presence,
  Thou home of peace;

To come into thy presence,
  Thou jewel of the clouds,
To come into thy presence,
  Thou jewel of the stars;

To come into thy presence,
  O Mother of black sorrow,
To come into thy presence,
  O Mother of the God of glory;

To come into thy presence,
  Thou Virgin of the lowly,
To come into thy presence,
  Thou Mother of Jesus Christ;

With lament and with sorrow,
  With prayer and supplication,
With grief and with weeping,
  With invoking and entreaty;

That thou mayest have me spared
  Shame and disgrace,
That thou mayest have me spared
  Flattery and scorn;

That thou mayest have me spared
  Misery and mourning,
That thou mayest have me spared
  Anguish eternal;

That thou mayest help my soul
  On the highway of the King,
That thou mayest help my soul
  On the roadway of peace;

That thou mayest help my soul
  In the doorway of mercy,
That thou mayest help my soul
  In the place of justice.

Since thou art the star of ocean,
  Pilot me at sea;
Since thou art the star of earth,
  Guide thou me on shore.

Since thou art the star of night,
  Lighten me in the darkness;
Since thou art the sun of day,
  Encompass me on land.

Since thou art the star of angels,
  Watch over me on earth;
Since thou art the star of paradise,
  Companion me to heaven.

Mayest thou shield me by night,
  Mayest thou shield me by day,
Mayest thou shield me by day and
                                    night,
  O bright and gracious Queen of
                                    heaven.

Grant me my prayer of love,
  Grant me my entreaty for shielding,
Grant me my supplication of pain
  Through the shed blood of the Son of
                              thy breast.

Count me not as naught, O my God,
Count me not as naught, O my Christ,
Count me not as naught, O kind Spirit,
  And abandon me not to eternal loss.

PRAISE OF MARY

Flower-garland of the ocean,
   Flower-garland of the land,
Flower-garland of the heavens,
   Mary, Mother of God.

Flower-garland of the earth,
   Flower-garland of the skies,
Flower-garland of the angels,
   Mary, Mother of God.

Flower-garland of the mansion,
   Flower-garland of the stars,
Flower-garland of paradise,
   Mary, Mother of God.

Sleep Protection

PRAYER

My God and my Chief,
  I seek to Thee in the morning,
My God and my Chief,
  I seek to Thee this night.
I am giving Thee my mind,
  I am giving Thee my will,
I am giving Thee my wish,
  My soul everlasting and my body.

Mayest Thou be chieftain over me,
    Mayest Thou be master unto me,
Mayest Thou be shepherd over me,
    Mayest Thou be guardian unto me,
Mayest Thou be herdsman over me,
    Mayest Thou be guide unto me,
Mayest Thou be with me, O Chief of chiefs,
    Father everlasting and God of the heavens.

THOU GREAT GOD

Thou great God, grant me Thy light,
   Thou great God, grant me Thy grace,
Thou great God, grant me Thy joy,
   And let me be made pure in the well of Thy
                                 health.

Lift Thou from me, O God, my anguish,
   Lift Thou from me, O God, my abhorrence,
Lift Thou from me, O God, all empty pride,
   And lighten my soul in the light of Thy love.

As I put off from me my raiment,
   Grant me to put off my struggling;
As the haze rises from off the crest of the
                             mountains,
   Raise Thou my soul from the vapour of death.

Jesu Christ, O Son of Mary,
   Jesu Christ, O Paschal Son,
Shield my body in the shielding of Thy mantle,
   And make pure my soul in the purifying of Thy
                               grace.

SLEEP CONSECRATION

I lie down to-night
With fair Mary and with her Son,
With pure-white Michael,
And with Bride beneath her mantle.

I lie down with God,
And God will lie down with me,
I will not lie down with Satan,
Nor shall Satan lie down with me.

O God of the poor,
Help me this night,
Omit me not entirely
From Thy treasure-house.

For the many wounds
That I inflicted on Thee,
I cannot this night
Enumerate them.

Thou King of the blood of truth,
Do not forget me in Thy dwelling-place,
Do not exact from me for my transgressions,
Do not omit me in Thine ingathering.
    In Thine ingathering.

I LIE DOWN THIS NIGHT

I lie down this night with God,
   And God will lie down with me;
I lie down this night with Christ,
   And Christ will lie down with me;
I lie down this night with Spirit,
   And the Spirit will lie down with me;
God and Christ and the Spirit
   Be lying down with me.

SOUL-SHRINE

Thou angel of God who hast charge of me
From the fragrant Father of mercifulness,
The gentle encompassing of the Sacred Heart
To make round my soul-shrine this night,
    Oh, round my soul-shrine this night.

Ward from me every distress and danger,
Encompass my course over the ocean of truth,
I pray thee, place thy pure light before me,
O bright beauteous angel on this very night,
    Bright beauteous angel on this very night.

Be Thyself the guiding star above me,
Illume Thou to me every reef and shoal,
Pilot my barque on the crest of the wave,
To the restful haven of the waveless sea,
    Oh, the restful haven of the waveless sea.

PETITION

Be Thou a smooth way before me,
Be Thou a guiding star above me,
Be Thou a keen eye behind me,
This day, this night, for ever.

I am weary, and I forlorn,
Lead Thou me to the land of the angels;
Methinks it were time I went for a space
To the court of Christ, to the peace of heaven;

If only Thou, O God of life,
Be at peace with me, be my support,
Be to me as a star, be to me as a helm,
From my lying down in peace to my rising anew.

I LIE IN MY BED

I lie in my bed
As I would lie in the grave,
Thine arm beneath my neck,
    Thou Son of Mary victorious.

Angels shall watch me
And I lying in slumber,
And angels shall guard me
    In the sleep of the grave.

Uriel shall be at my feet,
Ariel shall be at my back,
Gabriel shall be at my head,
    And Raphael shall be at my side.

Michael shall be with my soul,
The strong shield of my love!
And the Physician Son of Mary
Shall put the salve to mine eye,
    The Physician Son of Mary
    Shall put the salve to mine eye!

SLEEP BLESSING

Be Thy right hand, O God, under my head,
Be Thy light, O Spirit, over me shining.
And be the cross of the nine angels over me down,
From the crown of my head to the soles of my
                                            feet,
   From the crown of my head to the soles of
                                            my feet.

O Jesu without offence, crucified cruelly,
Under ban of the wicked Thou wert scourged,
The many evils done of me in the body!
That I cannot this night enumerate,
   That I cannot this night enumerate.

O Thou King of the blood of truth,
Cast me not from Thy covenant,
Exact not from me for my transgressions,
Nor omit me in Thy numbering,
   Nor omit me in Thy numbering.

Be the cross of Mary and of Michael over me in
                                            peace,
Be my soul dwelling in truth, be my heart free of
                                            guile,
Be my soul in peace with thee, Brightness of the
                                            mountains.
Valiant Michael, meet thou my soul.
   Morn and eve, day and night. May it be so.

NIGHT PRAYER

In Thy name, O Jesu Who wast crucified,
  I lie down to rest;
Watch Thou me in sleep remote,
  Hold Thou me in Thy one hand;
    Watch Thou me in sleep remote,
      Hold Thou me in Thy one hand.

Bless me, O my Christ,
  Be Thou my shield protecting me,
Aid my steps in the pitful swamp,
  Lead Thou me to the life eternal;
    Aid my steps in the pitful swamp,
      Lead Thou me to the life eternal.

Keep Thou me in the presence of God,
  O good and gracious Son of the Virgin,
And fervently I pray Thy strong protection
  From my lying down at dusk to my rising at
                                        day;
    And fervently I pray Thy strong protection
      From my lying down at dusk to my rising
                                      at day.

REST BENEDICTION

Bless to me, O God, the moon that is above me,
Bless to me, O God, the earth that is beneath me,
Bless to me, O God, my wife and my children,
And bless, O God, myself who have care of them;
    Bless to me my wife and my children,
      And bless, O God, myself who have care of
                         them.

Bless, O God, the thing on which mine eye doth
                         rest,
Bless, O God, the thing on which my hope doth
                         rest,
Bless, O God, my reason and my purpose,
Bless, O bless Thou them, Thou God of life;
    Bless, O God, my reason and my purpose,
    Bless, O bless Thou them, Thou God of life.

Bless to me the bed-companion of my love,
Bless to me the handling of my hands,
Bless, O bless Thou to me, O God, the fencing of
                      my defence,
And bless, O bless to me the angeling of my rest;
    Bless, O bless Thou to me, O God, the fencing
                   of my defence,
      And bless, O bless to me the angeling of my
                         rest.

REPOSE OF SLEEP

O God of life, darken not to me Thy light,
O God of life, close not to me Thy joy,
O God of life, shut not to me Thy door,
    O God of life, refuse not to me Thy mercy,
    O God of life, quench Thou to me Thy wrath,
    And O God of life, crown Thou to me Thy
                               gladness,
  O God of life, crown Thou to me Thy gladness.

THE DEDICATION

Thanks to Thee, God,
Who brought'st me from yesterday
To the beginning of to-day,
Everlasting joy
To earn for my soul
With good intent.
And for every gift of peace
Thou bestowest on me,
My thoughts, my words,
My deeds, my desires
I dedicate to Thee.
I supplicate Thee,
I beseech Thee,
To keep me from offence,
And to shield me to-night,
For the sake of Thy wounds
With Thine offering of grace.

Death Blessing

THE DEATH DIRGE

Thou goest home this night to thy home of winter,
To thy home of autumn, of spring, and of summer;
Thou goest home this night to thy perpetual home,
To thine eternal bed, to thine eternal slumber.

    Sleep thou, sleep, and away with thy sorrow,
    Sleep thou, sleep, and away with thy sorrow,
    Sleep thou, sleep, and away with thy sorrow;
    Sleep, thou beloved, in the Rock of the fold.

Sleep this night in the breast of thy Mother,
Sleep, thou beloved, while she herself soothes thee;
Sleep thou this night on the Virgin's arm,
Sleep, thou beloved, while she herself kisses thee.

The great sleep of Jesus, the surpassing sleep of
                        Jesus,
The sleep of Jesus' wound, the sleep of Jesus'
                        grief,
The young sleep of Jesus, the restoring sleep of
                        Jesus,
    The sleep of the kiss of Jesus of peace and
                    of glory.

The sleep of the seven lights be thine, beloved,
The sleep of the seven joys be thine, beloved,
The sleep of the seven slumbers be thine, beloved,
On the arm of the Jesus of blessings, the Christ of
                    grace.

The shade of death lies upon thy face, beloved,
But the Jesus of grace has His hand round about
thee;
In nearness to the Trinity farewell to thy
pains,
Christ stands before thee and peace is in His
mind.

Sleep, O sleep in the calm of all calm,
Sleep, O sleep in the guidance of guidance,
Sleep, O sleep in the love of all loves;
Sleep, O beloved, in the Lord of life,
Sleep, O beloved, in the God of life!

THE DAY OF DEATH

The black wrath of the God of life
  Is upon the soul of gloom as it goes;
The white wrath of the King of the stars
  Is upon the soul of the dumb concealments.

A perfect calm is on sea and on land,
  Peace is on moor and on meadow,
The King's joyful glance and smile
  Are to the feeble one down on ocean.

    Day of peace and joy
      The bright day of my death;
    May Michael's hand seek me
      On the white sunny day of my salvation.

Thou great God of salvation,
  Pour Thy grace on my soul
As the sun of the heights
  Pours its love on my body.

I must needs die,
  Nor know I where or when;
If I die without Thy grace
  I am thus lost everlastingly.

Death of oil and of repentance,
  Death of joy and of peace;
Death of grace and of forgiveness,
  Death of Heaven and life with Christ.

DEATH PRAYER

O God, give me of Thy wisdom,
O God, give me of Thy mercy,
O God, give me of Thy fullness,
    And of Thy guidance in face of every strait.

O God, give me of Thy holiness,
O God, give me of Thy shielding,
O God, give me of Thy surrounding,
    And of Thy peace in the knot of my death.

    Oh give me of Thy surrounding,
        And of Thy peace at the hour of my death!

JOYOUS DEATH

Death with oil,
Death with joy,
Death with light,
Death with gladness,
    Death with penitence.

Death without pain,
Death without fear,
Death without death,
Death without horror,
    Death without grieving.

May the seven angels of the Holy Spirit
    And the two guardian angels
Shield me this night and every night
    Till light and dawn shall come;

    Shield me this night and every night
        Till light and dawn shall come.

THE BATTLE TO COME

Jesus, Thou Son of Mary, I call on Thy name,
And on the name of John the apostle beloved,
And on the names of all the saints in the red
domain,
To shield me in the battle to come,
    To shield me in the battle to come.

When the mouth shall be closed,
When the eye shall be shut,
When the breath shall cease to rattle,
When the heart shall cease to throb,
    When the heart shall cease to throb.

When the Judge shall take the throne,
And when the cause is fully pleaded,
O Jesu, Son of Mary, shield Thou my soul,
O Michael fair, acknowledge my departure.
    O Jesu, Son of Mary, shield Thou my soul!
    O Michael fair, receive my departure!

SUPPLICATION

I pray Peter, I pray Paul,
   I pray Virgin, I pray Son,
I pray the twelve kindly Apostles
   That I go not to ruin this night.

When the soul separates
   From the perverse body,
And goes in bursts of light
   Up from out its human frame,

      *   *   *   *
      *   *   *   *

Thou holy God of eternity,
   Come to seek me and to find me.

May God and Jesus aid me,
May God and Jesus protect me;
   May God and Jesus eternally
Seek me and find me.

SOURCES

The verses on the pages of this book are taken from the following volume and page of the *Carmina Gadelica*.

Morning Protection: p. 13, 1.29; p. 14, 3.33; p. 15, 3.53; p. 16, 3.29; p. 17, 3.27.

Journeys on Land and Sea: p. 21, 3.195; p. 22, 3.173; p. 23, 3.175; p. 24, 3.185–9; p. 27, 3.191; p. 28, 2.317.

Work: p. 31, 1.233; p. 32, 1.237; p. 33, 1.271; p. 34, 1.267; p. 35, 1.275; p. 36, 1.289; p. 37, 4.99; p. 38, 1.295; p. 40, 1.309; p. 41, 4.97; p. 42, 1.311; p. 44, 1.315; p. 45, 4.103; p. 46, 1.319; p. 48, 1.325; p. 50, 1.329.

Charms and Banishings: p. 53, 3.319; p. 54, 2.169; p. 55, 4.169; p. 56, 2.45; p. 58, 2.69; p. 59, 3.57; p. 60, 3.37; p. 61, 3.235; p. 62, 3.241; p. 63, 2.95; p. 64, 2.95; p. 65, 2.105; p. 66, 4.119; p. 67, 2.91; p. 68, 2.99; p. 69, 2.109.

Encompassing: p. 73, 3.105; p. 74, 3.93; p. 75, 3.103; p. 76, 3.107; p. 77, 3.229; p. 78, 3.109; p. 79, 3.77; p. 80, 3.321; p. 81, 3.85.

Prayers and Blessings: p. 85, 1.23; p. 86, 3.63; p. 87, 3.177; p. 88, 1.35; p. 89, 1.55; p. 90, 1.101; p. 91, 1.103; p. 92, 3.313; p. 93, 3.73 & 75; p. 94, 3.205.

Festivals and Saints: p. 101, 1.163; p. 103, 3.111; p. 105, 3.117; p. 106, 1.135; p. 108, 3.159; p. 109, 2.167; p. 110, 3.157; p. 112, 1.187; p. 114, 3.149; p. 115, 1.107; p. 116, 1.107; p. 117, 3.143.

Moon: p. 121, 3.279; p. 122, 3.285; p. 123, 3.301; p. 124, 3.275; p. 125, 3.293 & 295; p. 126, 1.123.

Mary: p. 129, 1.27; p. 130, 3.119–125; p. 135, 3.135.

Sleep Protection: p. 139, 3.347; p. 140, 3.345; p. 141, 1.81; p. 142, 3.333; p. 143, 1.93; p. 144, 3.171; p. 145, 1.95; p. 146, 1.67; p. 147, 3.329; p. 148, 3.339; p. 149, 3.347; p. 150, 1.99.

Death Blessing: p. 153, 3.383; p. 154, 3.369; p. 155, 3.373; p. 156, 3.395; p. 157, 3.393; p. 158, 3.113; p. 159, 3.395.